FIRESHIP

FIRESHIP

EARLY POEMS 1964–1991

Peter Sanger

GASPEREAU PRESS
PRINTERS & PUBLISHERS
MMXIII

For Mary

What is time? When is the present?
RILKE

Rejoice in the dance
JEREMIAH 31:13

CONTENTS

— SEALSKIN —

— THE AMERICA REEL —

— EARTH MOTH —

— CODA —

SEALSKIN

1964–1983

Transit West

Water
hides seams
a keel
uncovers.

Birds leave
unmarked
passage
through air.

Endure
what you
know. No
oblivion.

Minims Towards an Equinox

Loose
yellow brick,
you heat
a hot
cricket.

Sail
to starwards
hauling
burnt
hemlock.

Not ice
or even air
snow
lightly
strikes.

Ticking
unpredictably
the red
kettle
cools.

Canti

Soft willow the whistle,
    woodcock.

Eats gnat and natters,
    barn swallow.

Catechism, cataclysm,
    blue jay.

Tucker, brackish clutter,
    black duck.

A scrape, escape,
    jack snipe.

Clack awl, clamour owl,
    crow.

Speak to me. . . . me,
    chickadee.

Bubble of braille,
    bobolink.

Trieste, tristia, triste,
    hermit thrush.

Tempera

Consider hands,
        how yours and mine
before they join
        reach blindly back
through quick and dead
        to Eden's earth
estranging touch
        when Adam reached
out hand for life
        before he lived.

Grace Notes

1.

Pamina,
this gift
of music
the night
before your
birth:

rain
steps a light
toccatina
over
windfall
earth.

2.

A swallow
cleaving
middle air
knows more
of you
than I.

3.

Fly fither
fret, spun
seed motes
and spools
spoked light
stalling
air.

Of Croft the Singing Light

I.

Lamp wick
            trimmed down,
trident
        of flame,
I
   cannot
            hear song
leave
     the wheel.

II.

In wheel's
            spinning chamber
a voice,
        footsteps
dance thread
                from the earth.
Petals invisibly
                form
a dark candle.

The Trout

(After René Char)

Banks cleft in facets
to fill the whole mirror,
shale where skiff stutters
from flow suck and push,
always plucked, ever
anchored reed,
what does your creature
become in clear storms
where heart has hurled it?

Homage to Georg Trakl

(Nähe des Todes)

I.

Alone a child lived
not alone.

The river had made him:

cliffs of red clay
pocked by swallows.

As a tree
he was waiting.

(Stone

turns the wrist
of a scythe.)

One tree hid
a wandering king.

II.

This is a spider
cold in the wall

who spoke with the moth
my sister
before she fell

whose wings
shed dust
and were still

who fled the long night
into fire.

III.

They nailed
my beloved
to a door.

Mutely
I entered
thorns.

IV.

Sibilance
stirs husks.

Listen
and forfeit
to sybilline
questing.

Watch me:
I smile.

Other Kingdoms

1.

Lips
and a leaf

touching
water.

2.

Lightly
we move

wind blown
wheat.

3.

Leaf,
and the rain
lightly beating,

a moth
alive
in your fist.

4.

River,
I enter
your silence

sealed
by the clasp
of your thigh.

5.

Walls
of soft chalk

sea-sprung
salt bitter lips

enclose me
withhold

sinking
through slow
tidal secrets.

Good Friday

Why shouldn't I learn
what others find
kneeling?

Centipede carries
a crescent
upon his head.

Worms of April
are chill
in my hand.

Fish a spring river:
spring
or fall?

Trout take the bit.
Their veins
run.

Frost

When snow eased pack
        off a spruce, my
animal head bucked
        away.

Inside every tree
        is a man needing
frost so badly, he'll
        have

to split out with a
        stick, at least
how I hear
        it.

For Edgar Murphy (1979)

(October 21, 1936 – October 6, 1992)

1.

A family of five after his
father's death to keep clear
of the Welfare, so Edgar
went into the woods.

At fourteen, he had his first
heart attack. Too bad it was
Christmas and so many trees
to sell.

He lay a dead side
in the snow while one
sister stacked and heard his
right hand chopping.

2.

The bridge washed
     out. He
gunned her
     across
the abutments.

Two wardens
     jumped into
the punt
     while he
took to water.

Escapes and
     such public
deceptions
     are his
way of dying.

The Lick

This brings them down
from the woods
           better than oats,

blue, a drilled cube
on a stake so
           horses can

lick all the honey
comb out, while melting
           ways in

through the salt
of another
           quick season.

Star-nosed Mole

Animals reach such
perfection we think
they can never die
like the mole my cat
killed to leave lie on
the diligent turf.

Too small, it looked brief
as a thumb, and how
could it shovel away
with such delicate
plankton for hands or
use an anemone nose?

Twenty-two pink fleshy
projections felt routes
through the loam
then neatly clamped
shut when this
frail eater found meat.

Bats

They have their affections
for earth as I saw when
one took the drop from
wherever it failed to go
hiding. Two dogs caught

it out on cement. No
help but to lift its keel
up on the apex which
grounded wings make, show
canines, show molars, show
all, while shrugging the bluff

of a lunge that would
topple it down unprotected
if made. The dogs fooled
a while with their fear
feinted pounces, grew bored,
allowed it to hop into dark.

Dancing Fox

This wasn't the one
I'd seen in a ditch
last year, riddled
by black and white quills.

This one was still on
the scarp where spruce
crops down into pasture
just back of the house.

Climbing his forepads
wherever they pelted
the air, he danced
over his bush.

Then neatly sat back
to watch the two
dogs in my yard
who stared up afraid.

Salamander

Two irregular rows
        of yellow spots
along a black back
        made it
common

and the water-filled
        jar propped up
by a wall where
        someone had
left it.

Nothing else could be
        done with four-
fingered hands
        than spread them
on glass

or with a short
        thick head than
butt slowly
        inside
at light.

Crosscut

Pushing
will buckle
its blade.

Two men
are needed
who'll pull

the teeth
through hand to
hand so

one swing
of its cut
nearly

ends where
the double
began.

The Man in the Woods

As if he were the only
one original he's almost
always called the man
in the woods. What other
names he has he needs
each month or so for his
mother living ten miles
up the road, who's sent
him orders to the crossroads
store for nearly forty
years, five dollars a time
for bullets, tea, tobacco
and one soda pop he
buys to treat his raving
sanity. Ask hereabouts
the reasons for his life
and you'll be answered just
as you've deserved, which
means your patience will be
tested, and your lies, for what
it is they've had to overcome.
Then the truth's out and one
which all damned fools would
guess but you: he's still stuck
somewhere along the line
a troop train started back
in Hitler's war. He watched

the track and when she took
a grade he slammed his window
down and hit the dirt to
rise up here still on the run.
He has a cave, they say, up
back behind the lake. Which
lake? There are two or three I
know about and more I don't
who've only seen the man but
once, while he pedalled a rusty
bicycle and I drove by.
That's when I saw his cap
of skins made from cats
he deadfalls in the woods. What
else I've heard could possibly
be true, like how he
visits friends and won't take
to a bed for fear he'll
undo his system. Instead
he packs his coat with hay
and lies down early in
the barn or finds a snug
place in the cellar. No
one I've met knows more
than you know now what
heedful instincts spur him
to his cave, while spreading
jet streams wave out overhead.

The Nature of Gods

"And should I not spare... that great city?" Jonah 4:11

1.

We seven in the cedar
        caul heard Laokoön's spear
            stab wood,

felt next the lift of levers, wheels,
        sharp rubble in a breach;
                four times we struck.

They heard a distant clash
        of swords, blade upon blade,
            but we still lived —

Ulysses; Thoas; virgin choirs
        leading the horse with garlands
            into their city;

craftsmen who cut, planed, caulked;
        dead Hector; Priam; Epeus;
            and I

all whirl, whirled by a stamp
        of the comedian,
            fatality.

2.

A worm in a peach,
    he loaded
        Leviathan's gut,

heard broken sea
    parted by slow
        caudal thrust,

then Jonah, he cried
    from the deep
        from the fishy belly:

"O Lord, hear
    this voice
        from the whale

confessing Thy mercy.
    Salvation
        is of the Lord.

I am Thy true
    whip. Scourge
        abject Nineveh

whose towers
      shall be pillows
            of dust."

Vertebrae flex:
      vascular tides
            still thrum.

Stone Animals

On the cup I was
given three deer are
circling the earth who
are circling it still
in a cave said to
keep those who find
it imprisoned. They
will know they must wait
for hooves striking
when all the stone
animals leap from
their wall to be what
we wished them
to be, the first time
we knew we were there.

Footfall and Shadow

Footfall
asked shadow
from where
he came.

Shadow
for answer
crossed earth
again.

Sealskin

I found a sealskin
     in a loft
and asked my mother
     what it cost.
She said the sealskin
     was not lost
my child.

I asked my father
     who had left
the sealskin in a
     seaman's chest.
He said it must be
     spoken soft
my child.

Your mother is a
          selkie queen
who wore that sealskin
          in a dream
until you were born my
          child of green
my child.

Now ask me not, I'll
          speak no more
for when the sealfolk
          swim near shore
your mother watches
          from the door
my child.

Dead Reckoning (1964)

> To live your life is not as simple as crossing a field.
> PASTERNAK

Ten weeks
snow covered
pasture creeks.

Wind fills
small gullies,
levels hills.

I discover
old senses,
recover

time, space.
Sight is useless
where each place

looks the same.
I must change
or turn lame

from stumbling
on rocks or
cold by tumbling

in streams.
The land is not
what it seems.

THE
AMERICA
REEL

1983

Steeplejack

He'd hid behind
hiding so much
he was good in the dark.

Sometimes he'd
shut both eyes
and climb
a ladder

of daylight
to be sure
the knack
still possessed him.

Smelt Shack

Give up what you
can't by building
a blue one or
yellow or red
with a stovepipe
to say when you're
safe, staring out
of the porthole
you've spudded in
ice, lining down
through the tide and
fresh currents while
sinkers bounce off
the dark sand
and your hooks seem
nearly asleep.

Crow In Winter

Just a bit more
and cold
might catch this
crow half wing
halfway across
slides
a glacier
left leaving.

It wouldn't be
any less
silent than
air is
now, that sound
of sealed
beak, stiffened
feathers.

Spring River

This river got tired of
the ice

tipped tabletops over
jammed

under the bridge and backed
itself

up in the fields to
gouge

a way through where
it flowed

before we gave out
the names.

Heron

Neck tucked in
like a sackbut,
      legs trailing

looser than use,
it shoulders a
      collop

of sky. Inside
is the man who
      tried

to enter its skin.
His skull sharpened
      down

to a quill point,
reptilian, curt,
      amber-eyed.

Courtship

A thousand feet outward
    and up three tumble
roll under, spin down
    through deflections, catch
back by a wing a tower
    that was almost conceded
build more and give all to
    the courtship. One screams
like gaffed metal. Two crows
    wrack over a hawk.

Slugs

Amputated, like thumbs
they seem stranded until
you go back, trace
them further, secreting
a sea where they track
less flexible mysteries.

The Snake

When I touched the green
        snake with my foot
two carrion beetles in
        shiny black coats patched
with orange ran out of its
        belly and showed me
expectant antennae until
        they'd made sure I was
warm. Then they dodged back
        to tidy and mate and
summon up newly hatched
        children with secret
slight rasps of their wings.

Calf's Head

Sentiment tossed it
in mud for dogs
            to strip:

eyes almost lashless
closed minutes
            between

our life, poll scrubbed
flat as a floor
            -brush.

Around the torn
neck, earth slowly
            mounts.

The rest from a beam,
gralloched, too hot
            for a knife

as after
sacrifice empire hangs
            articulate.

Trout Well

The keeper of trout in the well
          had to leave what
          little he'd built
with this shadow's reflection.

At dusk it's a pulse hunting
          down the fresh
          fallen and hatched
with nothing to add from its

unchosen circle of skylight
          and stone than
          measured
descents by clear water.

Ruffed Grouse

Nearly always the bird
      books explain how cock
partridge drum like a one
      lunger engine whose flywheel
drives up a broad piston
      to fall in soft sequence
first slowly then quickly
      as sparks almost catch with
the spin which bucks in
      spasmodic percussion to
silence, while I wonder how
      many remember a sound
which was mortal.

In Place of Gifts

1.

My kitchen is cold
and smells of apples.

What else do I have
but these five?

And a sixth to
swing me steady.

2.

Under the house
a spring

where butter kept
cool

and a granite slab
for cheese.

3.

A mouse skull, an
unbroken thimble

of bone, whose eye
socket I

copy with finger
and thumb.

4.

Along the high ridges, old
fence lines

and rabbit paths, a
fox

travels always against
the wind.

Spidell Hill

Under each vanished
        house a cellar of
fieldstone still holds
        down its field.

Water shrunk out
        of the ruts
leaves ice
        which breaks

at a finger's weight
        with the slight clash
of quartz knapped
        over the site.

The America Reel

Skye, 1773

A first pair
   began, each
set to one
   other, who
set to another,
   till all wheeled
around in step

   with each
other, in steps
   circling round
to dance for
   each other,
while lovers
   displayed

how sea spins
   around her,
how earth falls
   below her
whose wrist
   fills
a bracelet

the moon
wrought to clasp
    her, whose
hands loosen
    cords
a river wove
    round—

and nothing
    was scattered
that couldn't
    be gathered,
as circles
    of dancers were
broken alive.

The Staff

Earltown, Nova Scotia, 1824

After the first child had died
they walked out a day to find
somewhere pleasant to bury, level
and high, where soil in their hands
would give nothing back
but a hand's own stain.

It darkened. While others sat resting
Murray kept poking about,
listened, then lifted his staff
head high and drove it
to earth at their feet
saying: This is the place.

Recurrence swallowed occurrence.
Elsewhere a rod turned supple,
fell coiled, shed skin
the colours of earth.
Rhythmic with breath
its tongue cast forth.

They had to cope with the present.
A father offered his child.
Two farms gave ground
for the purpose, and having
been ordered, numbered,
their brief occupations began.

The Royal Series

A. & W. MacKinlay, Publisher, Halifax

At the top of the page
of her Penmanship book
she wrote as was bidden:

The month was October.
You must know the day.
Today is the twentieth day

of October, the ninety-fourth
year, just six years away
from what you'll not see

again, dear Christena,
who scribbled down Jessie
Bell's name, and Maria's

with nobody watching
then started her
copperplate course

with a *firm*, then a *may*
and a *yarn* and a *nun*
who was *muse* to the *tints*

on a *dune* where *Cain*
and the *emu* were *wind*.
So we gain the sad

urn with a song
in our *sark*, the wild
warp, the wild *warp*.

And in columns with
capitals flying: *Warsaw*
Vienna, Prague.

Storyteller

Then she began to fetch the right words back
with tell me a story now, that's what we
need to do. Tell me about the light which all
the old ones saw floating above
the Ross place up on Spidell Hill
and how Will Murray went to find it out
but came on back and wouldn't speak a word,
took to his bed and died. I saw that light.
I wasn't crazy then. And Dumpy's devil,
you knew him. He wasn't bad, no Dumpy
wasn't bad. He'd been a thief but hadn't
murdered anyone. One winter he took grippe
up where he lived, over on Spidell Hill.
Young Ferguson climbed there to help, found
Dumpy sitting crosslegged on his bed
eating a bowl of crusts and milk
when up he lifted, screaming out all his mush,
and fell back dead.
           So Sandy sent to
town to fetch the doctor in to certify
and when he had come went out to help
unharness. Then came a wind that blew
the hen shed loose and all the chickens
blew against the house and there was the devil
looking out upstairs, his face all barbed in flame.

They ran inside and stayed there overnight
and all night overhead it sounded like barrels
dropped and rolling. When they went up they
couldn't find a thing and nobody knows
why all of this went on, or if it had
before, since Dumpy's wife was quiet
and his daughter simple. I heard
it told by John George Ferguson, young
Sandy's son. He always said the truth. That's
all. You've made me up. It's time to say
goodnight. I'll keep below.
Old women don't need sleep.

Three Women

1.

Woman of husks
will you leave me
and sleep
in the standing corn?

You must break
the stiff leaf
of your skirt,
dance free

spilling
petals of starflower
you've
hidden.

2.

This woman
of wood had
unclosing
arms

on pivots
drilled into
her
shoulders.

Their swing
reached out
for what cannot
be held

until near
the end there was
nothing
but arms

overhead,
hands
quietly parting
the waters.

3.

Her head was
an apple
hung
on the tree

since last fall.
She was
watching my life
through its skin.

At last, growing
human, she
shrivelled
inside me.

Boneyard

Falls Cemetery, Colchester County, Nova Scotia

                                    Stones
tilt every way like wind cocked stooks,
but not as bad as he'd have expected
having to put back a pasture
wall the way it had to be each spring
for nearly thirty years. He couldn't complain.
He'd married land. Took what was best
of what there was to take and made it
his and then as she left stayed put
to pay her off.
                    The bone yard's how they name
this place and if you've made enough of what
they call a pile, you're meant to take some with you
into town and buy a decent plot up on the bluff
among the monuments. He wasn't asked,
but given choice he chose to make it here
with those not his, though theirs would rather not.
His dead ones all are under somewhere else
or possibly alive. Earth stops his mouth.
An empty flask neck periscopes downstream.

The Sisters

Kate & Betsy Murray: 1811–1901, 1816–1901

Later it would have been said
they'd had no right to be there,
one of them blind and both
too old to be living together
alone on the hill, where
no one should ever have lived
and no one lives now. The blind
will know how it happened,
the sound of a body which fell
and reaching towards it for what
wasn't there, the living, the sister,
who'd always been with her to see
and couldn't be forced to life
though she tried with her hands,
as God told her, until she felt
fire lost too, in the stove, and she
unable to start it for having
had matches kept from her.
The stove turned cooler to touch,
turned cold; and winter wherever she
felt came into the kitchen like someone
who'd entered with snow on his sleeves
and stood unspeaking.
Once, she opened the door and screamed
out to Baillie, her neighbour, across
two fields and a road.

He heard what might have been shouting
and went back inside, for what
could be wrong where people died
young, or died old with adequate warning.
The next day, or shortly thereafter,
a visitor came to find both
at the century's waning.

The Whalers

Though finding a whale
on a sandbank ought
not to happen, by damn,
it did in 1901
to Campbell of Earltown
and Spencer from
Highland Village.

They found it all
feeble in water not
deep as whales use,
and fraught with
a tactic scudded
for Bentley's
advice and his
tugboat, *The Susie*.

To kill the great
beast, they pierced
his side with a crowbar,
without much
avail, then hauled
him off free
on the tide. Alas,
the whale towed —

back down the bay,
Parrsboro way,
whose strength at last
failing they beached
at Moose Lodge.
Next day, another
whale joined him,
floating

in dead,
with a fifteen
foot shark
shovelling
herring inside her.
Useless for Bentley
to build
a planned fence

of admission.
The folk had arrived
from all over, from
Amherst and Springhill and Truro,
and nothing remained
to make money
but oil. Old
Morrison, whaler,

and Wadham cut
round a back fin
with axes, hitched
tackle and team,
skinned it out
like a tree stump, except
the chain parted and broke
Wadham's leg.

So ended extraction
and other interesting
matters: a cart, horse,
and driver who entered
the mouth of a whale
to have their photographs
taken, while others stood
whisky within.

For nature took
over and stank. The whales
yielded lastly
the most that anyone
handled, a world's
bleached structure of bone,
for seats in the garden
and gateposts.

The White Lady

Margaret Webster,
Chebogue Union Churchyard, 1819—64

After her death, he
imagined her life
as this motionless
dancing of form
into body, of
body to form
without sequence
extension or time.

Whether darkness
turned light or light
became visibly
dark as she entered
the silence he
kept, he couldn't
remember; but all
the gleaned fields

seemed to lie down
beside them. Her
voice was a cloak
lifting to cover
them both through that night
on the winnowing
floor, before each
ever knew

of another. Then
waking alone
with her absence
he made it
this likeness he'd
married without
having seen her,
asleep upon

alien sheaves, wheat
loosely caught
at her waist, with a
sickle which almost
falls clear of her hand
holding back
into marble.

Jerome

Sandy Cove, St. Alphonse, Nova Scotia, 1864–1912

One must have taken its mouth to the light
as you'd lift up a horse's hoof, felt
in for the tongue while Albrite told over
and over how he'd found whatever
it was propped by a beach rock with tide almost
reached where feet should have been.

It was stub, hooded over, blunt carcass,
but dry, unslickened, and as he'd got closer
turned human, legs cut off trim at the knee,
stumps sewn tight, beside it
a tin box of biscuits, a can filled
with water clamped into a heelmark.

This lay on the couch where Albrite and Gidney
had brought it, watched them and slowly
became what they knew, as much in those minutes
as they'd ever know of what he had been,
done, endured, almost nothing
and silence, no more than the pain a nerve has

after what it existed to service
is severed. He ate what was given
and slept and after some weeks chose a sound
or was chosen to say it that gave them
the name which was needed to tend him,
Jerome, as they heard it, or agony

working out through to something they took,
which he let them keep. They moved him
along the French shore where he lived for fifty
eight years and spoke only twice with anyone
near to report it: one year he whispered
Trieste, as his homeland, then later

a third name, *Colombo*,
the ship which had judged him for innocence,
guilt, betrayed or betraying, as murderer,
victim of what he'd committed
or kept from, witnessed inside
by his implicate silence and ours.

Tuberculosis House

Whoever lived up here where earth
and air are both too thin is said
to have died of it. Even in summer,
wind jumps across the fields
like a cat in the snow. A freestone
chimney left won't stand as some
assuaging monument.
It's still the same flue of wind,
not warm enough for broken lungs
and those who hadn't the money
to go somewhere else and die.

This is no naming of places.
Places are always named,
forgotten, remembered
by an old man who
dies one year before I find him.
This is to see a place
among hips and haws and wild run
raspberries and the cast iron cooking pot
that seemed intact, rim up, until
I dug loose and found it eaten back
contained by what earth contains.

The Voyage of the Saladin

Valparaiso, Chile, to Country Harbour, Nova Scotia,
February 8 to May 22, 1844

The *Garnett* and *Belfast* refused.
Only Sandy Mackenzie would offer
him free passage home aboard
the *Saladin*. How much could
Fielding have told him? As much as
was needed might nearly have been
the truth to play on Mackenzie's
pride at having sailed through to
the final voyage before he retired.
Fielding, slack blackguard,
had failed. Been pinked
in the shoulder resisting arrest.
Lost his ship and locked up in Callao
for trying to smuggle out guano,
escaped with his son George's
help, and hid down in dock trash
for two days and nights
til some captain or other took both
back to Valparaiso
with charts, a few clothes
and the forfeited *Vitula*'s Bible.

Hours out for London they started.
Each captain was too much alike
not to think the other a fool.
The crew heard their quarrels out twice,

once through the door
of their cabin, secondly
secretly told them by Fielding
to sailmaker Jones, a stump-legged
cripple from Clare; to Trevaskiss,
a red-headed man who'd deserted
the *Constellation*. Beau Hazelton watched
with full bright eyes and the Swede
tried hard to follow. When Jones first broached it
this Anderson shouted: "By God,
I will take a knife and cut his throat.
He'll no more strike me back
from the helm." And silver, the
silver she carried. Fielding had touched it.
They'd spent it, spent over
so often they dreamed of white
hands scaling silver.

Just after midnight
Bryerly, first mate, fell ill.
He lay down to sleep on the hen coop.
A hammer, a broad axe, a maul
and an adze were kept in the stern
of the longboat. Trevaskiss could
handle an axe. He split the first mate
while Swede with Beau Jack

stepped after Mackenzie below.
His dog scared them off. They crossed
to the half-deck to whisper
the carpenter up. As he cleared
a hatch, Anderson hammered
him home. The fools threw him over
too lively and up sang shouts
of blue murder. Fielding cried
loud to cover, but it took place
too quickly Mackenzie up there
on the deck in his nightshirt
ordering the helm swung down
turned bloody with hammers but not going down,
wouldn't go down, until Fielding
chopped clear with his axe,
young George shouting on,
and Mackenzie dropped over the rail.
The rest played more easy. A fresh
watch was called. Moffat trimmed sail
as he died. Anderson axed Jem Allen
staling off in the sea,
then followed Sam Collins onto the head,
beat him down through.

It was Sunday. All day alongside
sharks slowly turned showing
milt white bellies. There were two
still living, untouched, Will Carr,

the ship's cook, and the cabin boy,
John Galloway. Carr wakened
at six, saw blood by the foremast.
They ordered him aft to the poop
where Fielding, George Jones, Trevaskiss
Beau Jack and the Swede were waiting.
The Captain explained it: their master had
left them alone. Carr looked at the sea,
at the boats secured in their places,
heard: "We've finished off
Sandy. We'll have no more cursing
and swearing. We've finished
the carpenter, mate, Moffat, Jem Allen
and Sam. Will you join us?" Carr
fell to weeping while everyone
swore (but for Fielding) he wouldn't
be harmed, they'd wearied
of killing. Most all of that day
Carr cried with fear. He cried
as he cooked them their breakfast.
Young Galloway laughed and wished
he'd been given a cut.

Fielding made over the watches
and shaped a course northwest by north,
towards Newfoundland. He ordered
the cutlasses, guns, two hatchets,
the broadaxe, the adze, and a large

iron hammer cast in the sea lest
the crew become jealous.
One gun was kept to shoot fowl.
All hands took rum in the cabin
and it being sabbath, Fielding
suggested observance. Each man
kissed the *Vitula*'s Bible,
swore loyal and brotherly love
for each other. That settled, they eased
into laughter, bragging which man
murdered best. They'd done it too
well for Fielding
who slid to draw
Galloway in: he ought to kill Carr,
Jones, Trevaskiss. Before
he could answer, Fielding had gone
to search Anderson out: kill Carr,
kill Galloway, Jones and Trevaskiss;
and back to Trevaskiss: Galloway,
Carr, they'd be poisoned. Carr
heard him inside the pantry
loading the gun by touch in the dark.
Trevaskiss uncovered two pistols
hid under a table.
They pried the lid of a chest
which Fielding had locked, found
a carving knife missing since Sunday
and brandy they judged to be poisoned.

Fielding was decoyed below.
Accused, he denied, offered rum,
called them cowards, turned to climb
back on deck. They fell on him
screaming, gagged him and roped
hand and foot, then debated his life
into death while he listened.
Hazelton, Jones, Swede and Trevaskiss
made Will Carr and John do the last deaths
for everyone's safety.
On Tuesday, at seven, Fielding climbed
gagged, hands bound, to the deck.
John Galloway wouldn't go near.
They forced him to touch Fielding's
body. Carr and George Jones
threw Fielding away from the stern.
Carr spoke to John and explained
how one lives, how one dies. Together
they captured young Fielding
who held onto Galloway's clothes
as he went overside, while
the crew advised shaking him off.
This was done and the murders
and guilt thought sufficient.

After thirty-five days, sails set up
to the royals, their ship struck
Saladin Point. The crew

tried a muddle of stories: dead captain,
drunk mates tipped loose from a yard
and everyone drunk
until Jones stove the casks.
But the charts, Fielding's clothes and his son's
wouldn't fit without passengers
left to explain them. Taken off
and let free, the crew seemed
to wait for arrest. All confessed.
Anderson, Jones, Beau Jack
and Trevaskiss were hung by
a thoughtful device which made
their four drops simultaneous.
An assemblage, gathered
to witness, watched
with greatest propriety. Galloway,
Carr were acquitted, having
acted under duress and begun
the confessions. Galloway vanished.
Carr went to Digby. He walked
at a trot, drowned remembrance
in liquor each April, and that's
all we know at the end, except
Fielding tossed over the stern as if
evil itself were bound, gagged,
and cast out and the vessel kept
running before the wind, for they
couldn't do more, save cover

her name up with boards ten days
before striking, while Anderson
painted her figurehead white,
a black and gold turk of bronze
painted white, its eyes cataracting,
retracted, diminished in whiteness,
sealed down under white to a place
they'd never imagined, past murder
and death, where nothing they'd done
was not, and they were what was done.

The Old Place

Seeing it as it was is more
than anyone can do
who tries to see here now.
One door hangs halfway off,
another's flat and lifted
uncovers slugs in cauls of ooze.

Inside, it's confirmation
of all that can be hoped,
smashed, thieved, emptying
out from room to room
as you walk through and up
the stairs with one hand

to the wall. A starling
wrings its throat, bucks
through the ceiling laths. What's
left is what there was
from inside out, three elms,
a brook, a field, the track

which brought you here,
and then this touch of cold air
feeding up from where the cellar
holds smelling of stone
and wood turned back to earth,
which you ease down to find.

Gaelic Cemetery

It's said or almost
all been said, until
the living leave
their living dead.

A Garden Kalendar

Selborne, Hampshire, 1788

I. THE BEE BOY

Bees were his food
and sole amusement.
In winter, he dozed

by the fireside,
torpid. In summer,
quested for game

through fields on
the sunny banks
or slid

in a beekeeper's
garden rapping
on hives, snatching

his prey bare-handed,
sucking the honey-
bags out.

His lips made
a noise like buzzing,
but save in this

favourite pursuit
he showed no manner
of wit,

for those of his caste
possess seldom more
than one point of view.

Later he moved
to a distant hamlet
and died before manhood.

2. OWL SONG

A neighbour of mine
who has a nice ear
remarks how owls

near this village
hoot in three different
keys: G flat or

F sharp, in B flat
and A flat. Query:
do these dissimilar

notes proceed
from three different
species or

from individuals?
The notes of our
one specied cuckoo

are mostly in D.
But two sung together
in D and D sharp

which made
poor concert.
Nightingales

sing in rapid
transitions.
Perhaps in a cage

in a room, their notes
might be brought within
steady criterion.

3. THE FIELD MOUSE

Out of the hotbed
of dung leaped
this grotesque:

a white-bellied fieldmouse
with three or four
young clinging by mouth

to her teats.
This instance of tender
attachment might daily

be matched by monstrous
perversions in nature.
For swine

dogs and cats will eat
their own offspring
which owners have handled

too freely. I leave
such events to
abler philosophers.

Telescope

It lies interlocked in your hands
compact with things it has held, extended,
holds nothing, then fills back inside
from where you direct it to see—
horses and ships, hills, trees, stars,
two does and two fawns stepping
a freshly ploughed field from furrow
to furrow.

               Outside, coherence
is shaping to enter the lenses
which must by reversal turn small,
and you, if you're quick, will spy
glints from silica spectra
detached at the eyepiece, where
what was left watching still serves.

The Rat

I stooped to
untie
a sack full
of carrots
when Edmund
Iago or Gloucester
jumped out,
was whalebacked
with fat
running over
the shelf, leapt
walls of dead
pots banged down
as I struck
with a broom
at an oozing
away underneath
where saucers
of poison set
forth did
the trick overnight,
turned
shoulders to grass
incisors
renascent
here in the dark.

Baroque Variations

The flies do rise again
       from little graves in walls
dancing awhile in air.

For heat from the stove
       is mother to their
resurrection, the stock

of a new refreshment
       they fray
at the pane

to tell there is life
       within, and without
a flat light

of snow impelling
          them back
to a coldness fled

as this, a continuing
          stay between heat and light,
stills over again

to crisp husks
          on the sill.
And variously named

are the cities
     for which their
ambrosias bled.

Frog Bait

A hand dropped into
the pail felt
cool, felt moss

the nudge
of quiet bodies
escaping

as far as they could
around their tin pit.
To catch them

was holding
slack leather-
gloves

whose fingers
were suddenly
felt

frail bones
pushing back,
busy

as lips
at the hook
which stapled

shut
as we lowered
away

on the line,
children
still learning.

The Vault

Waking this morning
to wear my body
I found it still
breathing and warm

as if someone took it
last night, running hard.
What reason
there was

I'd no right to offer
who had followed myself
down below
to a vault

near the sea
which was empty
fish smelling
and thought

how others lived there
where I have to live,
as across he
came running

the child in his
blindfold, whom somehow
I'd gathered
to save.

Burlap Sack

It smells of itself
and whatever was
in it: apples,
potatoes, cod.

Shaken flat it
lies on the floor
with nothing
hidden.

Then rises to swallow
the lot, would take
the whole world
to heart

hang by
the neck, one
ear cocked,
bulging with secrets.

One I held once
in a dream
wrung its
tippling imbalance

alive, inside out
on my hands
and became
phosphorescent

aqua marina,
the luminous
cell
which began.

The Gravel Pit

Peel back the world's body,
you'll skim
the first scree.

I pushed something once
as a child that shovelled,
rammed

what yellow machines
have scooped from this pit
for keeps.

It was space, gavelled
back, Hadrian's
Wall

freeways and flyovers
out to the road not taken
towards which

there travelled
in convoy
my mud-coloured

staff car
and sprocketed
carrier of Brens

whose cleats
of worn chain
spin round.

Post Digger

Searching for words to sort analogy out
    he tells me of rocks in the pit, light
as a handful of dust, of one tossed at him to catch
    that shattered in flowers, shells, leaves, hooves
—trilobites, ammonites, sprays from the petrified forest
    growing beneath us, bones, scales, corals,
roots, lustres—and how he must live with the whole
    western world gone crazy on credit, and no one to buy
up his pulpwood. He cites an auction last week
    where a quota fetched more than pedigree cattle.

On this side, his hill slides under in sand.
    He shows me a post hole augered six feet,
point four trillion years, and I sketch
    the horseshoe crab which spawns on Japan
and some degrees south of his province.
    He's heard it's still living, resembles
what's down in the mine. Scorpions, spiders survive,
    as would the cockroach, perhaps,
storms of vortical fire.
    He thinks the socialists start them.

Marrakesh, 1965

Among the Mercedes
buses squadroned
in Meknès and Fez
I saw
indigenous culture:

Tribal theatre. Two men
took turns at great
journeys, riding on
each other's back as a boy
with a drum beat hooves.

Dismounted they
shouted as needful,
while drumbeats
steadied the palfrey
that year of another war.

Bombay

Let us praise
        this brown man
whose fingers
        still work

on his hands
        extracting
from fresh,
        hot dung

a cab horse
        has spilled
on the curb
        bright grains

which feed him. So,
        dying is
never
        quite wasted

and life
        as we know,
must always
        prevail.

Killing Ground (198—)

Frogs ruckle and cluck
        from pasture seeps.
Owls glimmer back, whoop
        on the opposite hill.

Books explain how it
        happens. I've read
until it seems luck
        to survive by design.

Descending ascents
        through the stem, sidereal
charts swung into place
        above the Americas

trigger the flocks
        which fall one by one
as antique assassins
        revive.

The Meeting

Since accident had brought him there
it almost seemed right to hide and watch
the other hack at something twisting
through a field.

            Pity might be what kept
the watcher quiet. Or else he held back
from being caught in limits accepted too late
to share with anyone.

            A shadow displaced
still followed him that way, watching
the watcher hidden in his wood,
another,

            coveting neither, who'd recognized
both in the face of illusive division
reflected by water.

Windscape

From no certain quarter
but fluent, cross-purpose
to precedent set by
its own contradiction
as suddenly doubling
or tripling or more
it forces again, again
at one side, then sucks
itself back into stillness
spills but to baffle
broken by sounds of
contention that leaves
tether to make;
and long notes
sequacious as motion
lifting, falling
in Clevedon and Concord
diversely on strings or
set at the lip of a flute
tremble to thought, though
stricken, thrice circled
the singer stare mute.

The Ancestors

Here was a stage where I stood
    with earth clothes upon me
watching the celebrants dance
    a court dance as they'd danced
it for two hundred years

around the cloaked woman who
    toyed with a midget beside her.
Left double, right double
    leaned me their duplicate mocking
to choose from, and I

knew the dancers were watching
    unaged in the dance they exacted,
created from patterns I still
    had to follow, by truth
and refracted illusion.

Behind me three Ghibelline towers
    flared in soft flame
which set the stars singing
    or birds, as I woke
to light through the window.

Poetic Justice

The publisher* asked for a preface explaining themes. This postscript is a compromise. Its position might retain some of the advantage a poet has in not explaining. But a demand for explanation has its right. A poet must ask what is meant and hold himself accountable for its implication and consequence. He must also listen to the meaning of sound. Otherwise, he had best keep quiet.

Opposite the house where this is being written rises the first whaleback ridge of Spidell Hill. On top of it is a circular pit, about fifteen feet in diameter. The pit is almost filled with hundreds of lichen-scabbed rocks of equal size and weight, no larger and heavier than what somebody strong could carry in each hand. It has some of that quality of inappropriate fixity most of man's abandoned workings collect after fifty years. But no one now can say if a house, barn, tip, mine, or some other thing man committed were ever there. If you look at the pit again, it shifts from the human to the natural. You hear the buckle of tectonic plates, see small meteors falling unconsumed through a thinner sky, and the accurate litter of a retreating glacier. The pit really exists on a margin where natural and human history overlay each other, where strict definitions become impossible.

There are the same shifting margins between inner and outer, exile and kingdom, will and necessity, politics and

---

* Lesley Choyce at Pottersfield Press, the original publisher of *The America Reel*.

innocence, immanence and transcendence. Doubles could be duplicated without limit, within certain limits. Poetry can use all five senses (not only sight), and a sixth one, to mediate justly along these margins. Such mediation is what this book attempts.

Like other arts and all the rooted crafts, poetry must have licence to reply to the test in seeming riddles. This is the only way some questions can be answered. Despite post-Darwinism, for example, Thoreau's comment of 1856 still stands: "What sort of philosophers are we, who know absolutely nothing of the origin and destiny of cats?" Blake's answer, from the forests of the night in 1794, confirms our need for riddling replies.

When Helen Creighton collected old songs in Nova Scotia during the first half of this century, she asked her singers a similar question to find Scottish ballads like "Lady Isabel and the Elf Knight". "Do you know the one about the milk-white steed?" That question a reader and listener should ask a poet, and a poet must ask himself.

EARTH
MOTH

1991

What he could do he did. Watching him, it seemed as if a fibre, very thin but pure, of the enormous energy of the world had been thrust into his frail and diminutive body. As often as he crossed the pane, I would fancy that a thread of vital light became visible. He was little or nothing but life.

VIRGINIA WOOLF, *The Death of the Moth*

Skipstones

You gave them to me
    by telling how you
and your father walked
    where the river
    still furls

in routs, rucks you sorted
    for this one, which one,
alive in its bias to free
    ravelling staccatos
    from water.

The Colours

This is the boat
you untied
each morning
which rowed

past the beach
and the island
rowed left
over

scatter, stipple,
lilies and
striders
confluent

with frogs
to go back
into yesterday's
secret

still white
on the canvas
and here
for you

all the years
later:
umber, vermilion,
green.

Picture Blocks

Twenty still left, unable
    to make any pattern.
The children who stay
    play with vanished companions:

hands reaching up to catch
    what must be imagined, or wave,
or touch, or warn. A swan swims
    its headless passage over

scuffed water while two slanted
    racquets reach for a shuttlecock
knocked away clean to glory.
    The children who stay watch

with androgynous calm,
    fragments mismatched,
perfections
    who almost existed.

Sampler

As the dream ended, each thread
in its world became supple
and warm where she stitched, worked
into light across water's shuttle.

A horse and no rider clipclop
across the bridge home; trout flicker
like leaves adjusting their
shadows, and all the flowers quicken

to sunlight, silk starlight, the light
of a balanced moon, pattern
from pattern repeating, frost
flower to feather, green fern,

all entering the fable, heart's ease
or provisional Eden,
where pippins still hang
and Jerusalem only was golden.

Earthenware Bowl

Tilted to fill with light
    it gives back the first ever
moon you hid as a child
    in October.

No-one could dance with its weight.
    Children might try
and smash the whole thing to layered
    deposits, clay, fire, milk

spilled among burrowing shards
    like an ultimate
judgement the righteous
    always expected.

Outside, it's earth, patched
    with a russet
coat, circled by
    seven scribed rings

chafed away almost to essence,
    except where the touch
of your hands completes
    their circumference.

Basket

Whatever's well made
    stays irrevocable
does it? This basket
    for one, interlocked.

White ash to your touch,
    its every weft under
leaps over and finds
    what checkerweaves follow.

What else must be carried?
    Bread, flowers,
some children to raise,
    while they still want you.

Litter

Cat, and two
kittens, calico
curry

pranking
in three ways
ply

homeward
one way
together.

September,
all visitors
gone.

Snow-Wright

Fox, deer, finicky
    nick of mice in snow:
a man walked ahead
    with his dogs, whistled
them close, allowed one
    to wallop abroad
within reason.

So this is design.
    Some feathered away
to find it, tracks
    holding back by a step,
subliming their dance
    to return as shapes
of fluent resistance.

Fisherman

The bait is himself
pretending to be
what he's not, afloat,
adrift, plucked
cleanly up to drop
where water is quickest
or slacks back off
a rock. Casts
improvised from each
other, rolling, loop,
slide, enough for
conditional yieldings
terror must fight
with itself, strike
into drier light.

Earth Moth

Asked to say
how it's done, she
told me to watch

with stillness and
silence, apparent
indifference, look

elsewhere at
something beyond
where I looked,

use the edge of
an eye, and kneeling
she lifted a dun-

coloured leaf from
its drift rigged
by diagonal veins

holding frayed
segments which slowly
adhered into

wings, and this moth
where we're
somewhere apart.

Silver Thaw

Move, and the glitter cracks
    in brittle confusion. Boughs
spring clear of their loss to
    flex parabolic curves, trip
what they touch until
    the whole stand almost dances.

Sounds circling out chase
    what followed before,
not rest, but histories of silence,
    lengthening, levelled, failed,
perhaps expiation,
    no doubt in a limited place.

Collocution

Hector Saint-Denys-Garneau, 1912–1943

Shrike in his cage of bone,
a thin bell singing, slit
with the usual concision

before there was time to take
out each word, partly fill
it with light, tell it: *Look*

you are almost human; I
nearly forgive you. I know
you must also die

like the sound of that flute
I set in the wind's throat.
And the word's black script

fell away, flying back
on the water, whose
river rose in him and broke.

Escalade

Paul-Emile Borduas, 1905–1960

Tell him of apples, roads, friends
the kingfisher's clatter and clang
of a pillaging jay. Quote words

he once offered: *Wasn't I born
too soon, in an immature country?*
Use his stream's transformation

as trope, its planes skewed aslant, their
foldings, slidings wrinkled as wind
ruffles up and boats he'd rather

have built patter lightly as paint
drops: *Let suicide cease in
Canada to be sole honest*

*solution to the tragedy
of our poets.* Schismatical
brother-in-arms, he could nearly

convince all but the absolute
mad, and his paintings condemn
the rest to castles in Egypt

return of the imprisoned sign,
flight of ephemeral dancing,
catacombed rock sunk in wine.

Solipsist

Laying his head in the heart of earth
to hear eft and emmet, interpreting
blithely a psalm by his brother worm,
he regrets you're the voice he can't play,

an obstinate *thou* refusing to shift
to demotic, objecting a *why*
which means he's not understood.
And yes, you almost believe him, his flows

of benign explanation which proffer
you both absolution if only you'll
jump right in, drift off to Pointe Au-Delà,
where he can keep wordlessly singing.

Plagiarist

He's that best friend you'll never quite have,
the confessional double who shares
every secret and has to forgive
as if you're above betrayal.

Sympathize with his difficult life,
its whirligig jig of feculent
snouts he knows how to cherish,
impossible now to keep going

as time passes by and he'll become
the back number, unless he has found you,
cloaked in transcendent cliché, alone,
half-coherent, and utterly no-one.

Simoner

His life is, of course, miraculous,
fresh waves to skim, confected cook-ups,
and now the latest bathetic. His eyes
almost give him away, avoiding your

own to find others he's able to see through.
A confederate man of council, committee,
league, he's ape to the emulous, pander
to purse politicians, or multiple

if you wish, with a throne of fabulous
mirrors he'll sell at his own choice price.
Light-footed he was when Dante saw him,
inverted and sucked by flame.

Lapidary

A man of conventional vices
fraudulent, proud, a false witness,
he often sells lies considered
quite finished, remembers a lot,

not some great ball of crystal no-one
can lift, but a wink of unseizable
light flittered under the water
whenever he'd leaned to drink.

His hand in that spring had gripped
hidden displacements, shutters which slid
thickened translucence concealing
whatever was there, prismatic, plutonic,

a speck of evading refraction
which held nothing back and almost
something he'd seen. *Quartz*, he said later,
and learned how one usually means.

Crow Court

Out on the ice an anthracitic glitter
fetches him close to look at his first
protagonist, a hunch of loose feathers,
a wing attempting to fly, another

dark legend from earth before his peaceable
kingdom. Around its picked carcass a strut
of ambiguous tracks makes patterns
of neat execution as if the old fable

were true and crows kill their cannibal
kings. Walked around, he walks round,
in a measure of ultimate equity.

Properties of Wood

John Thompson, 1938–1976

1.

A language of leaves and water
   was what he intended, words shaped
clear by commonplace things, helves,
   shafts, tines, strips of interior bark
suppled and woven for sieves and baskets,
   ladles, tubs, all manner of tackle
trimmed to form by his knife, a ship's
   keel crook, carving out workable space.

2.

Escaping from madness, he named
   particular things, *cambium,*
phloem, xylem. The Greeks had brought gifts.
   Grains running straight and crooked
eddy like water, taper away
   into root. Cut, they catch light,
breathing it back as suffusion.
   The dark wood is heartwood.

3.

By touch and smell in the dark
    he could name them, bluntness of elm
that shreds when the wedge splits,
    oak with its weight of old metal
hidden inside and birch feeling
    packed as a fetlock. Maples rive clean,
polish in air into nutshell
    and float either dry or green.

4.

He made his choices for music
    of a width, length, thickness cut
from only one board. If struck
    they are different, vibrate at various
quickness. Two men in a wood for sound
    must rap each tree with an axehead
till one hears resonance ring
    out through the mast tip.

5.

Each tree is an ark. Oak, spruce,
    birch, juniper (while it still lasted)
were all driven down on the tidehead,
    bent to one purpose, pinned
by a play of sapwood in seasoned
    holding the cambers firm.
Instress, outscape, whatever
    they make is deciduous.

6.

He'd found a book for their attributes:
    acacia, *immortal*, and almond,
the favour of God. Firs may excel
    in virtuous patience, but the apple,
still evil, or life? Thorns must be
    reverenced. Fits of symbolic
taxonomy, easy to mock
    given the cost of fidelity.

7.

Lost in the vesper forest
 he plucked a twig from a thornbush.
Its wound issued blood, his voice
 saying: *I who hung with the kestrel*
seek justice. Those who maddened me
 living now market me dead.
Plagiarists, frauds, let the makers
 denounce and forgive them.

8.

His is the trunk of green olive Ulysses
 left rooted below him, hewed
off its branches until he'd erected
 a pillar, wimbelled and matched it
with three massy columns, then webbed
 all together with thongs of crimson
ox-hide. That bed was the sign
 by which Penelope knew him.

Silver Poplar

So is isn't is. It is: a
negative game, apophatic,
turning to rights inside out.

I'd rather watch riddles
of leaves duck when the wind
hits like a flock of, you know

the kind, black on the back,
white as they veer away. I
wish you'd remember their name.

Alewife Run

What from a height is
easy intelligence following
clear from its source is check
to them, choice, feeling for
currents which drop into
darkness or bolting thin
on a rift. Schools work by,
dorsals tacking
the surface as if uncertainly
purposed until you step close,
with a shadow which scatters them
loose, reflections repeating
reflection, zigzagging
tails, scales, spun free
a moment, flipped back
under cover, flanked
for contiguous journeys.
Gravel is spongy. Water
thickens with spawn as a reek
draws predators down, ripe
in their way, and open.

Gordian Worm

Also one of the threads,
hanging a drift
of adjusting curves cast

to keep leeway in water,
it's a bit, fibre, straw-coloured
hair which can never

be fixed as a yoke knot.
Straightened, it sinks, leaving
no trace in the sediment.

Crane Fly

Up on six legs, astraddle,
a filament gantry, it hooks
the gauze curtain till

wind shakes loose then
jigs away off the wall drily
clipping right back to begin

at the curtain again. What
your hand might allow could be
pity, compassion, or not,

and the silence you clear
either nothing at all or
some sound you couldn't quite bear.

Grey Seal

Chuff-headed, hoving from wave form
to fall, it watched us, waited, as
if we were the expected, some

curious couple with patience
enough to observe when it plumb-
bobbed under, slid up in silence

an apposite distance away,
intercepting our shadow where
grains ran against, wind hurled sky.

The Rug

Fleur-de-lis or luce, Christ's
mother and the common day,
the French king's tent, his broken

flag, and Vala still crowned
in Havilah, where the gold
of the land is good and there is

bdellium and onyx. You've watched
how they flower on the ground,
fair, fresh in their flourishing

out of a green design
delighting, lilies of field,
simple meadow lily.

Wind Storm

Everywhere the trees are falling
    echoing fallen, helmeted
spruce, canopied arcs of elm,
    birch struck to bone, rowan
releasing its berries, sinewy
    hornbeam cracking slow torque to die.

Everywhere the words are failing,
    echoing fallen. Tentacular
cities, mighty at heart, lie still,
    and the tongue in its glory
summons old strains of omega
    as rivers glide back to fire.

Next Session

Forgeries, lies,
    alas resolutions,
pity lives out
    its last years.

Business as usual.
    States insist
on their ends
    like equations:

this, being this
    is another
solution, or else
    no solution.

Committees
    in charge of our
deaths live
    them out here.

Minute Men

This is the place of weapons.
They send their children to school,
return them at night.

They are tested to dream
without madness, fixed
with immaculate tubes.

Coupled, they slide down silos,
have freedom to shoot
each other in cases

of aberration. Cruising
across the Dakotas, they
vent a kingdom of light.

Airspace

It likes being held:
    dependence of skin
on metal, webs, snaps,
    dials to take up
the slack when weight
    spews off on target.

Abstractions flick over
    its screens from some
distanced explosion.
    Bright star, you have
darkened, created,
    provisional, dead.

The Intestate

Now you can prove
where his innocence fails,
how an age he fled
invokes your infections.

You can name what
he tried to ignore
when silence licensed
murder: he fed

upon hatred, arranging
his self-destruction.
You will live better,
wreathed for illustrious

death, nor hear
the same music, in air
under earth, as a god
abandons the capitol.

Sea Bones

Gather them up as a father's wreck
not coral and rich and strange
leached to parched metamorphic,

latticed trabeculae honeycombed out,
split cylinders plugged, blunt ovoids,
clasps, cusps, shafts, fretworks of vertebrate

piercing, slight spatulate parings, dry
shards sheered down under sand,
but the cup still tastes of clay.

The Web

Walking to find the world
as if it had never
existed, weighing wind

light, thought, the centre
an orbweaver circles,
crossed silks running counter

continuous net, clear
threads that converge
by divergence, we were

touched by a filament
catching us both,
an invisible weft

our hands carried
to tear when
transparency lifted.

Hatch

Flight of the swallow sleighting
    middle air, festival
tilts, rare turns obliquely
    scything, fricative chat,
that twittering in the skies.

Lift of the mayfly drifting
    nightfall's arbour,
practical coupler, eclogue
    or tappeting fleck,
to feed earth and the ravished.

Kestrel

So much for its stiff-quilled stoop,
its beak's obstetrical slash,
grandeurs, foiled, counterfeit voices,

the wince of surrogate violence
gripping a shape into earth.
Kestrel keeps clear, the name

and the cry it makes, *killy*,
buff, slate, hover of kingfisher
wingbeats converting to flight

away, fall, flared back and stalls
on a tree tip, wings
cockered shut that instant.

Crabapple Blossoms

Light, and light's duplicity,
  they flaw in a scud, haul
juddering back, snubbed,
  sway halt and sounds
of dark water, song sparrows
  lucent by water, shake
each loosening spray.

2.

Conclusive of nothing, themselves
  most of all, their scent is
a trace of the rose
  become new, staying old, a play
of immaculate presence, stone
  being stone; wood, wood;
blossoms, blossom.

3.

White, pink under white
    where the calyx held. Wind away now,
earth remains as a promise. How
    much is enough? All there was:
blossom unfailing, its
    whiteness falling,
wherever you break to touch.

Wordsworth's Dream

Light sea dark, riffle
of air to work with,
waves quickly pitched:

sleep, a cupped shell,
silence inside it,
multiple, menaced,

obscure, which every
wave makes, falling back
releasing another.

Wasp's Nest (Winter)

Lifted, it leaves
the weight you expected
    becomes
a carton of air.

Hamlet might hold it
and turn to his soul
    saying
thus. The moral keeps

various, and when
torn apart shows two
    facing
circles of cells, pocked

like a sunflower's
seedhead. What can be
    fastened
around your bones when earth

comes to take you-
this featureless
    creature
of paper, peeled

in delicate strips,
or a memory of
    plundered
sweetness emptied?

Talus

Astraea's groom and Artegall's,
the trig automaton in Spenser's
dream of absolute justice

who in his hand an yron flale
did hould threshing out
death *by way of enterdeale*

for *finall peace and faire attonement*,
he models a new Platonic style
in antiseptic comfort,

lasering light, testing out deft
neutronics, competent
with our main communal art

forms, detached, never bored,
a modular pragmatist
trained to look after the end.

Burnt Land

Stub, stump, stock, anonymous slash
and burn, fit for the age's idiom.
Think how it probably roared,

flame-outs crowned up in the rampikes
tossed top to top down from the hill,
then the whole valley imploded.

Ash on the air's still alive where
sunlight strikes it, and fireweed preparing
some serial coda, insisting magenta.

Strawberry Box Lantern

Midsummer's eve, an older dark,
    and you might collect six pine
pint boxes, counterpoise tops;
    cube space in a centre and square
an hexagonal star. Beg

a candle from where for the box
    at the bottom and light your way
back through that night when you were
    a child, swinging *Look, my own light.*
It's been such a very long time.

White Fawn

Out of the darkness, white,
shapeless, a shifting
resisting the headlights

it stepped slowly, stopped, stared
back, was what never
would happen believed:

white fawn from waste forest
and valley, all things
by its form signified,

man, lion, ox, the last one
becoming an eagle,
and nothing was broken,

destroyed. Great secrets,
clearness, a grace
which balanced to tread

on four winds, middle kind
and a maker. Men came
the next day, shot it dead.

Windlestraw

Windlestraw, withered,
wind-shuffled, your weight
is a breath on my hand,

hollow, an emptiness
centred, fire slowing
down into stain,

dun-coloured, broken
and breaking, stems
softened loose

by rain. There were
times I expected
you'd light me

beneath where earth
becomes age. Too late
for oracular

voices, too soon for
posthumous
dreams, only forms

sliding back into bodies
ascend
the blackening grain.

Leonardo's Lyre

Take what Vasari described
as *mostly of silver, in form
    like a horse's head*

and how can you play it now,
except as a dream or the shape
    of a dream's shadow?

Credo, credente, credulo,
dismantling their final
    trio

assert what love in the void?
A voice perhaps
    vanished, a reed.

Candlelight

Once was a night we'll
make up some history
   of fire

its crepitance first,
then silently
   formlessly

flaring until it has
almost burned
   out

gutters back tapping
catches which
   stubbornly

carry and slowly
flames seemly
   tipped by

transparency's vertex
while all the king's
   children

turn O into almond
ovaling its shape
   from air.

Woodcock Feather

As light as whatever you wish,
some fostering fall, perfection
of snow or the tiptapping brush

of a leaf. November, and look
we're still here. I've thought
how we once broke cover, our quick

double flight shaped out
of moss and grass, leaving
this scapular feather. Soft, is it

slate? Is it ash? Grey, my love,
shading to rufous, a form
interfusing, allusive:

spreckled, barred, streaked, a gather
of mottle and margin, or touch, or
breath we also have drawn together.

The Sleeper

1.

Under again, fallen through, this time
an aperture's eye whose lenses
unlapped as he dropped, darkness from

dark, down through the pit of his body
to retinal night where gold almost
glittered, glinted a hovering key.

2.

At last a quiet well in the wood,
abracadabrant perhaps, at least
some partial salvific. He kneeled

at its lip, listened down. Wings beat
back clear of part pinioning,
semaphored out, black, black, white.

3.

On the track between trains, after
something to kill, that boy he was
did it, crouched to re-enter

his life. He'll kill it again.
Something's blood stains a leaf
inside a crystalline stone.

4.

Moth wings and caddis, spent chrysaloid
chambers, silk cases and chitinous
dust spilled loosely before him, served

up. So this was the meal of the dead.
Alive in his dark, quickly dying,
he spoke to thank her he loved.

Luna Moth

One I saw once in time, delicate
    scarf of green, fresh as bruised mint
    and marked by a lintel's lamplight,

acidulous evanescence, mauved
    on its forewings' fore-edge,
    wreath of colourless blood

which I've carried inside me too long,
    evading its silence, avoiding
    to ask if anything

ever existed, imago and image
    returning as things in themselves,
    forced to a perfect stage.

Black Mirror

Inside it is always night,
darkness receding, depthless,
and images living a life that isn't
substantially theirs but
memory's saved from oblivion.

The same world's outside
a night window and doubles
your face staring out
staring in at the room
which almost surrounds you
with chairs, an old table,

a lamp you like to keep dim
for shifts of travelling shadow,
while this reflects daylight
returning, those contexts which change
and revive from continual death
across its bituminous surface,

estranged, disembodied,
patterns of rainbow and cloud,
stabilities carved out of water
flowing from intricate night,
ecstacy, pain, incompletion
as light assumes dark.

Mare's Skull

Here in its skull your fingers touch
the language's stubborn structure.
This was a flange of air, and this,
one of water; there, the dry bone
of earth simmers green flames
as moss re-kindles its surface.

Through crook and strait a lost time
recovers its ritual, eyes
close their sockets, breathing draws out
up its throat, and a dream becomes
foal in your arms, both in one,
its skin a sweet smell of bran.

Bone in its muzzle of water,
darkness harnessed by light, earth
unexanimate run their green
fire through the fields
like horses ridden by blood,
or still, intuit what holds.

The Wish

Firefly or falling star
    crossing the darkness,
indefinite light
    slight as earth's shadow,
particle into which
    all colours gather,
gone, or night stays.

CODA

2012—2013

Log-Slate

Twenty to forty years after they were written, I think of the poems in this book as sailing on their own course, one laid out by a master, not by the writer, on a heading that will fetch them up in a port I can never visit. They sail not some *mare nostrum*, but a *mare sonans*, the sounding sea surrounding this world with the voices of animals, birds, insects, trees, grasses, winds, waterfalls, glaciers, rivers and other ardours, including those of humans. Among the cosmogonel sounds of the latter are small volumes of poetry and music, perhaps magnified at the distance of the moon by their concurrence with some greater harmonic coherence.

Seafaring, like poetry, is an art of memory and judgement. One of the qualities I look for in poetry is that it be yare. The adjective, and its adverb form yarely, are obsolete now. Yare means ready, prepared, alert to act quickly to secure order and continuance. By no accident, the word survives at present in the lexicon of *The Tempest*. One of the effects of any art is to preserve, sometimes in dormition until occasion and necessity awaken them, subtleties of accurate meaning. Yare is used by the Boatswain during the play's first scene to point the cogent, urgent commands he issues while Antonio's ship (of usurped state) seems about to split apart (lose its metaphorical integrity) because of the storm Prospero has conjured. The Boatswain appears once again in *The Tempest*'s last scene to describe the ship as "tight and yare and brav'ly rigg'd," ready to return to the mainland carrying Prospero back towards his rightful kingdom where, as Prospero says, "Every third thought shall be my grave." Yare, then, is a condition both of staying afloat and accepting the condition of human mutability.

Yare was the measure by which the poems in the first section of *Fireship* were selected from three never to be published books I put together between 1964 and 1983. Excluded from this section are poems that became part of *The America Reel* (1983). Two poems from these years not reprinted here did eventually appear in two later books. "Shahrazád," written in Iraq in 1965, found a place in *White Salt Mountain* (2005), and "Banbury Cross," written shortly after I began living in Nova Scotia in 1973, appeared in *Aiken Drum* (2006). I have dated two of the poems in the first section, if only to indicate that its poems are not arranged in the chronological order of their writing. The section was put together as a sequence foreshadowing the sections which follow it in *Fireship*. Like Richard Outram, I believe a book can be a labyrinth whose centre is the journey to itself. A concerto grosso, not a singular declamation.

Less needs to be said about the second section of this collection, *The America Reel*, and the third section, *Earth Moth*. In the text of *The America Reel*, I have corrected typographical errors and trimmed the concluding essay, "Poetic Justice," of its bibliographical acknowledgements. A word in "A Garden Kalendar" has been altered. *Earth Moth* remains unchanged.

Both books were written while I lived (for fourteen years) in an isolated farmhouse among the Cobequid mountains in north Colchester County, not far from Earltown, Nova Scotia. Coming after my living, sequentially, in England, Canada, England, Australia, England, Canada and various places within them and in between, Nova

Scotia has been the only home where circumstance and choice allowed me to stay more than three years. I dug in: the area about the old house, its history, and the memory and survival of those who had lived or then lived close to it, are part of the subject of *The America Reel* and *Earth Moth*. During this time and for twelve more years, I also taught technical writing, library skills, scientific and agricultural history and the literature that was once called natural history at what was then the Nova Scotia Agricultural College in Truro. The poetry was a manner of understanding both where I lived and how I made a living. In some ways, a matter of manners. I could not write easily or quickly. And dates of publication can be deceptive. It took two years to find a publisher for *The America Reel* and nearly three for *Earth Moth*. The latter might not have been published had it not been for the support of the late Douglas Lochhead. I name him here with deep gratitude.

All the poems in *Fireship* concern where we were, where we are, where we will be. I use the second person plural here carefully. These poems are, by intention, autobiographical only tangentially. Their autobiography is intended to be more like that of a ship's log than of a confessional diary. Anyone who has spent time on a well-run ship's bridge will know that what are called reckonings—where the ship was, is, and will be—are primary. Reckonings, objectively observed and expressed, are the ship's biography and context (just as they are a poem's). Reckonings are not only the ship's bearings, its compass direction, past, present and future, but also the condition of the sea and the direction and force of the wind. Necessary alterations to, say, the sails might be construed as an autobiographical implication involving judgement, decision and disciplines of skill and character; but such acts also concern adjusting to elements of wave and wind other than, greater than, the personal.

The journal log on a sailing ship was ultimately the master's responsibility. The master could correct and add to it. But if a poem is like a ship's journal log in its commitment to telling what really happened, it differs from that log by having no consistent master to correct or add to its entry. Prospero may appear to be a consistent master, and he has, at times, been characterized as such in modern variations upon Shakespeare's play. But at the end of *The Tempest*, he asks the audience, as his master, to release him: "Gentle breath of yours my sails / Must fill, or else my project fails." Borges had similar, unillusioned balance when he wrote in his essay "Poetry" that "We change incessantly, and each reading of a book, each rereading, each memory of that rereading reinvents the text." If that is true, the reader or listener is closer to being master, not Prospero. Each reading or hearing is the log of a different journey, with its own obligations and privileges, and, in turn, its own audience.

And the poet? I would not look for the poet's analogue in the figure of some master. The poet's intention and performance may be polyphonic, but only through riddles of grace may they speak in all voices, at all times. I would look for the poet's analogue in the figure of the chief mate, the position in modern terminology held by the Boatswain in *The Tempest*. He or she must try to keep the driving of the ship, with its crew, yare.

It was the first mate on a sailing ship who had responsibility for recording each twenty-four-hour's ship's reckoning on the log-slate that served as the main source from which the ship's journal log-book was compiled. The log-slate's entries may have been in a sense preliminary, but they were not tentative. As Richard Dana remarked in *The Seaman's Manual* (my copy is the fourth edition, dated 1849, and was published by Edward Moxon, the publisher of, among other poets, Wordsworth, Coleridge and Tennyson), "nothing should be entered which the mate would not be willing to adhere to in a court of justice."

I have a log-slate. It dates from the second half of the nineteenth century. It is the size, even to its thickness, of a laptop computer. It looks like a leather-bound folio, but instead of being bound in leather it is cased in pine. The two pine boards which bind it are held together by two small brass hinges screwed into what in a book would be called the spine. The pine boards were painted brown but the paint has been worn through in many places, worn by salt water and handling. The paint is also scored by the marks of old navigation. When closed, this log-slate must have been used as a table upon which to rest nautical charts while they were scribed, pencilled, ruled, plotted. Traces of compass circles, course lines and triangulated plots have struck through into the soft pine in the same way words are marked by the pressure of negotiation we bring to bear upon them.

Opened, the boards become backing and frame for two black slates, on the left, on the right. The left hand slate is plain. The right hand slate is roughly scratched into a four column grid like the pages of an account book. These columns were used to record such entries as the time of observations, the speed of the vessel in knots, the depth of water under the keel, the courses steered, the direction of the winds, the vessel's leeway (sideways drift) and any pertinent observations (probably on the blank, left slate in expanded form) such as the general conditions of sea and weather and the sighting of other vessels. When made at sea, all entries were recorded according to nautical time, running from noon to noon, not according to the shore time of what was called civil computation, from midnight to midnight. Neither is the timing of poetry the timing of prose. On the log-slate the first mate's word was bond.

Adze, sickle, scythe, flail. Sextant, dividers, parallel rules, protractor, compass, seven day windup chronometer—and log-slate. As they fall from our computerized fingers, the symbolic imagination, which helped human beings invent them and which familiar use had dulled, returns. And their performance has never vanished completely. Fiddles are still made by hand. The Royal Canadian Navy still employs sextant sighting, celestial navigation, watches on the bridge and what are called paper charts in parallel with radar and global positioning as emergency redundancies. If satellites were suddenly kicked out of orbit and the screens darkened, some travellers would still know where they were, are, will be. There would still be slate reckonings. Yare.

As mineral, slate is static sediment composed by the earth's surface weight. Slate is a version of ancient sea as persistent as the æonic deposits of language. It was precursory to paper when paper and other writing surfaces were rare, not easy to make, expensive and re-usable only after difficult renovation. Slate's delete key is a wet rag. It could, although resistant to the wash of a wave, be wiped clean, rubbed out, but became immediately afterwards expressive to the slightest human scratch of chalk. That quality is one of the undercurrents of Mandelstam's "The Slate Ode," written during the preliminaries of Stalin's dictatorship in 1923, in which "the language of flint and air" is also the language of "flint and water." Fifteen years later, Mandelstam would end, or begin, his voyage in the Gulag. His crime was writing poetry, one of the haven-finding arts.

The persecutors and murderers of Mandelstam, if they were more than opportunists, must have regarded themselves as agents of civil order and poetic justice. But I doubt whether their private language for the occasion was so elegant. I suspect it was phrased as Mandelstam getting what he asked for, getting what he had coming, getting cut down to size, getting his. Getting his what? Death. Such are the euphemisms of power. Ironically, their techniques of incomplete statement and colloquial self-exculpatory realism concede that there is a finer language of truth and justice. For Mandelstam did not call down on himself a levy of poetic justice. He was poetic justice. I remember a fragment of Herakleitos: "Justice will overtake fabrications of lies and false witnesses." Its sentences are in the air we breathe, the water we drink, the bread we break, the seas we sail, the words we end. Blank, slate offers itself again as a chartable reckoning of night.

Fireships

Orient fireships draw
out to sea. How brave
are their elements, brave

as Achilles' shield, and yet
they are paper, books
we never had time to read.

Each carries a candle. For
a moment its flame
is balanced on water.

This one's the black ship death.
No surprise. That one is rose.
It glimmers like Renoir's flesh.

The third is green. It almost
turned into leaf, but was caught
before it could re-assemble.

You ask how I know. I don't.
Trust the great sail
of metaphor. Each

intends to complete
the world, no sailor left
to watch mute sea.

Notes & Acknowledgements

The Rilke quotation used as one of the epigraphs to *Fireship* is taken from Lou Andreas-Salomé, *You Alone Are Real to Me: Remembering Rainer Maria Rilke*, translated by Angela von der Lippe (Rochester, NY: Boa Editions, 2003). ⟨ The epigraph to "Homage to Geory Trakl" is the title of a poem Trakl wrote between December 1912 and February 1913. An English translation is "nearness of death." Trakl died of a self-administered cocaine overdose on November 3, 1914, having suffered a nervous breakdown after tending to the Austrian wounded during the battle of Grodek. ⟨ The epigraph to "Dead Reckoning" is based upon the translations by Max Hayward, Manya Harari and Henry Kamen of "Hamlet," one of the poems at the end of Pasternak's *Doctor Zhivago*. ⟨ Sources for the stories told in several of the poems in "The America Reel" section are listed and discussed in that book's original edition, *The America Reel* (Halifax, NS: Pottersfield Press, 1983). Three of them perhaps need re-remembering here. The dance set in the collection's title poem was described by James Boswell in his *Journal of a Tour of the Hebrides*. The theme for "Baroque Variations" was first played by Bishop Jeremy Taylor (1613–1667), and the poems of "A Garden Kalendar" are centos based upon passages in Gilbert White's *The Natural History of Selborne* (1789). ⟨ The epigraph to the "Earth Moth" section is from Virginia Woolf's essay in the collection, *The Death of the Moth and Other Essays* (London: Hogarth Press, 1942). ⟨ "Black Mirror" owes a debt not only to a window in an old house but also to a passage in

Alfred North Whitehead, *Dialogues of Alfred North White-head*, recorded by Lucien Price (London: Max Reinhart, 1954), p. 192. In it, Whitehead's wife, Evelyn, discusses a black-backed (rather than the usual silver-backed) mirror hanging on the wall. She says, "My black mirror is the world of memory. And what the poets are able to do with words to save these intense moments of ecstasy or pain from oblivion is a black mirror." ⟨ The essay "Log-Slate" uses quotations from Jorge Luis Borges, *Seven Nights*, translated by Eliot Weinberger, introduced by Alastair Reid (New York: New Directions, 1984), from Osip Mandelstam, *Selected Poems*, translated by Clarence Brown and W.S. Merwin (London: Oxford UP, 1973) and Philip Wheelwright's *Heraclitus* (Princeton, NJ: Princeton UP, 1959). ⟨ Some of the poems in this collection originally appeared in *The Antigonish Review*, *Dalhousie Review*, *The Fiddlehead*, *The Globe & Mail*, *Grain*, *The Malahat Review*, *Pottersfield Portfolio*, *Poetry Canada Review*, *Prism International*, *Queen's Quarterly*, *Satadal* (Melbourne, Australia), *Scrivener* and *Tributaries: Anthology, Writer to Writer* (Ottawa, 1978). ⟨ *The America Reel* was first published by Lesley Choyce at Pottersfield Press in 1983. *Earth Moth* was first published by Susanne Alexander at Goose Lane Editions in 1991. The original edition of the latter was designed by Julie Scriver and won an Alcuin Society award for excellence in Canadian book design. ⟨ I thank all the editors and publishers who helped and trusted this work. ⟨ Thaddeus Holownia generously made the photographs for the book jacket and the essay. ⟨ *Fireship* is dedicated to my wife, with love, joy and reason.

PETER SANGER

⟨ Gaspereau Press acknowledges the support of the Canada Council for the Arts, the Department of Canadian Heritage (through the Canada Book Fund) and the Nova Scotia Department of Communities, Culture & Heritage.

Typeset in a digital revival of Centaur & Arrighi by Andrew Steeves & printed offset and bound under the direction of Gary Dunfield at Gaspereau Press, Kentville, Nova Scotia.

1   3   5   7   6   4   2

National Library of Canada Cataloguing in Publication

Sanger, Peter, 1943–
Fireship : early poems, 1965-1991 / Peter Sanger.

Includes: American reel, and Earth moth, as well as two dozen unpublished early poems.

ISBN 978-1-55447-121-8

GASPEREAU PRESS LIMITED ⟨ GARY DUNFIELD
& ANDREW STEEVES ⟨ PRINTERS & PUBLISHERS
47 CHURCH AVENUE, KENTVILLE, NS B4N 2M7
Literary Outfitters & Cultural Wilderness Guides